EAL
Pocketbook

By Alice Washbourne

Cartoons:
Phil Hailstone

Published by:

Teachers' Pocketbooks
Laurel House, Station Approach,
Alresford, Hampshire SO24 9JH, UK
Tel: +44 (0)1962 735573
Fax: +44 (0)1962 733637
Email: sales@teacherspocketbooks.co.uk
Website: www.teacherspocketbooks.co.uk

*Teachers' Pocketbooks is an Imprint of
Management Pocketbooks Ltd.*

Series editor – Linda Edge

© Alice Washbourne 2011

This edition published 2011.
Reprinted 2012, 2013, 2016.

ISBN 978 1 906610 30 2

E-book ISBN 978 1 908284 75 4

British Library Cataloguing-in-Publication
Data – A catalogue record for this book is
available from the British Library.

Design, typesetting and graphics by Efex Ltd.
Printed in UK.

Contents

Foreword

Britain today is culturally and linguistically diverse. One in eight pupils in secondary schools speaks a language other than English; in primary schools it is one in six. In inner London over half of all pupils speak another language and over 200 languages are spoken in London schools. However, many EAL (English as an additional language) learners in the UK – and in 2010 there were almost 900,000 in total – join schools that have little or no previous experience of teaching pupils whose first language is not English. It is no longer just an inner city issue.

Some EAL learners have been in the UK for five years or more, or may have been born here. These are the majority of EAL learners in British schools and are often known as advanced EAL learners, although their fluency in spoken English may mask continued needs in understanding and in using more academic forms of English.

Diversity brings richness to ways of thinking, being, seeing and saying. It has resulted in the fusion and creation of new styles, music, language and cuisine. For teachers of pupils learning EAL this can be an exciting environment to work in. It can also create challenges to make sure all pupils can thrive in their learning.

Foreword

For many pupils learning EAL, language can become a barrier to learning. They are learning English at the same time as learning *through* English. In addition the home culture and norms may be different from those in the school and of their peers whose first language is English.

As teachers, we are committed to ensuring that we provide the educational opportunities for all of our pupils to succeed. We know that learning English and feeling welcome are the keys to success. However, it can feel a little daunting to know how to include an EAL learner and teach the English needed in our subject or curriculum alongside the prescribed programme of study or syllabus content.

Foreword

Whether you teach in a multicultural setting or in a rural area with few EAL learners, this book is for you. It will:

- Show you how to create a welcoming learning environment where pupils can see themselves reflected
- Help you to develop their English language skills in the context of learning in any subject
- Describe a range of practical approaches and strategies that you can use in your everyday lessons

Extra, Extra

Why Extra?

EAL pupils are learning English as an **additional** language, not as a replacement for their first language. English is an extra. There are cognitive advantages to being bilingual, but only if both languages continue to be developed. So, as teachers, we need to support EAL learners to develop their English but also find opportunities for them to use and learn in their first language. (More about this in the next chapter, Welcome to our Worlds).

In *this* chapter you will find information on how an additional language is acquired and see a range of profiles of EAL learners. You will be helped to find your way around the sometimes complex terminology and clarify some common misconceptions about EAL learners.

Who are EAL learners?

An EAL learner is a pupil who was exposed to a language other than English during early development. This means that an EAL learner may have been born in the UK.

EAL learners are not a homogeneous group. They come from varied backgrounds and parts of the world and will have different experiences of education and English. They may have come to the UK as a positive choice or they may have been forced to leave their home country.

'My name is Yuki. I am ten. I come from Japan. I am living in Oxford with my parents because my dad has a two year contract to work with a big company here. I had a private English tutor in Japan and can read and write a little but find it hard to speak and understand when people talk to me. My parents want me to learn fluent English.'

'My name is Hassan. I am 8 years old and I live in Bradford. I came to the UK three months ago. I came from Somalia with my mother, 13 year old brother and six year old sister. I don't know where my father is. I didn't go to school in Somalia. My brother speaks English but the rest of the family don't. I am a Muslim. I am good at football.'

More EAL learners

'My name is Ali. I am 14. I come from Afghanistan. I speak Farsi and Arabic and understand Pashto. I came to the UK alone. Both of my parents are dead. An uncle helped me to escape the war and come to the UK. I live with my foster family in South Wales.'

'My name is Mohamed. I am 15. I am from Eritrea. I speak Tigrinya but don't read and write it. I can read Arabic. I lived in Holland for three years and am fluent in Dutch. I think Dutch is now my strongest language. I came to the UK from Holland with my family four months ago.'

'My name is Anna. I am Polish. I am 11 years old. I came to the UK with my mother for a better life a year ago. I live with my mum and English step dad in Norfolk. I did very well at school in Poland and always got top grades. I speak Russian and Polish. My dad is Russian and still lives in Poland. I visit him in the school holidays.'

'My name is Shazna. I was born in London. My family are Bangladeshi. I am five years old. I don't speak much English because we use Bengali at home, and where we live our family, friends and neighbours all speak Bengali too.'

Some definitions

You may have come across a range of terms used to talk about EAL. It can be confusing! Here, and on the next page, are some common terms and definitions:

EAL	**English as an additional language.** Can be seen as more accurately describing speakers who may speak several languages and who are also learning English.
ESL	**English as a second language.** Sometimes used instead of EAL, but not seen as accurate as it doesn't recognise the multi-lingual abilities of many pupils.
TEFL	**Teaching English as a foreign language.** Describes a context where speakers are learning English, often in their home country, for specific purposes such as study, career, travel or pleasure.
TESOL	**Teaching English to speakers of other languages.** TESOL courses are designed for post-16 and teach general English to adults for practical purposes such as to access health and other services.
Refugee	A person who has had to leave their country and who is afraid to return there. A person with refugee status is granted leave to stay in the UK for five years.
Asylum-seeker	A person who declares themselves to be a refugee but whose claim is not yet determined.

More definitions

Isolated EAL learner	An EAL learner who is learning in a school and setting where few (if any) other pupils share their first language; language acquisition needs; ethnic, religious or cultural heritages.
Bilingual	A pupil who has access to two or more languages. The term does not imply any particular level of fluency. Tends to be used to describe EAL learners in primary school settings.
First language	The language to which the pupil was first exposed during early development.
Community language/ heritage language	The language of the heritage country. It could be the official language of education, rather than the dialect spoken at home. Often a distinction is made between modern foreign languages studied as part of the school curriculum and 'community languages' which may be studied outside of school hours.
Advanced EAL learner	Generally refers to an EAL learner who has had five or more years' exposure to English and who is fluent in conversational English.
New arrival	A pupil who has arrived from another country, often at a time other than the usual September transfer date.

How long does it take to learn an additional language?

A good question!

The length of time taken to learn an additional language can depend on many factors, including age, attitude, personality, motivation, aptitude, learning environment and level of fluency in the first language. It also depends on how you define being fluent in a language – fluent enough to chat with friends, or to give a formal presentation? Just in speaking and listening? Or in reading and writing too?

Research shows that it is possible for a newly arrived EAL learner to learn conversational English in two years. This level of conversational fluency is described as having *basic interpersonal communication skills* or BICS.

However, it may take longer for a learner to become proficient in using academic language. It can take five or more years for an EAL learner to operate on a par with their monolingual peers. This academic language proficiency is known as *cognitive and academic language proficiency* or CALP.

Rates of learning an additional language

The diagram below shows the rates of language acquisition of a native English speaker and an EAL learner. You can see that it takes much longer to be fluent in the English needed for success at school.

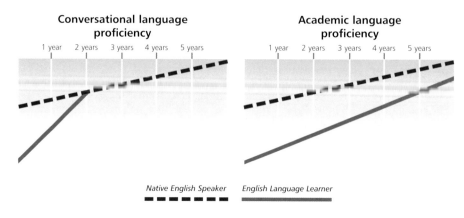

Conversational language proficiency

1 year   2 years   3 years   4 years   5 years

Academic language proficiency

1 year   2 years   3 years   4 years   5 years

Native English Speaker   *English Language Learner*

What's the difference between learning your first language and EAL?

Younger EAL learners go through a similar process to children learning English as their first language. They make similar 'developmental errors'. For example, they over-generalise, as in '*goed*' rather than '*went*'. They are both still learning about the world.

EAL learners often start learning English later than at birth and they usually use different strategies because they already 'know' a language. These strategies change over time. A five year-old will not use the same strategies as a 15 year-old.

There are greater differences with older students, whose first language is more developed. They may be literate in their first language and speak, read and write in other languages. They are at a higher cognitive and conceptual level of development than children first learning a language.

Younger children often pronounce words like a native speaker, but older learners have more knowledge and understanding of the world and language awareness. For them, learning English is the learning of new labels for objects, ideas and concepts. Therefore they are likely to learn English more quickly.

Dual iceberg model

The diagram below shows Cummins' model of bilingualism. He envisaged bilingualism as two icebergs, each representing one language. The tips of the icebergs show the features of the two languages that are visible. It looks as if the languages are completely separate. But if you look beneath the water you see that they are not stored separately in the brain.

Cummins sees deeper levels of thinking skills underlying language. This means that concepts can be transferred from one language to another. If a pupil has learned something in one language they can access the knowledge in learning another language. The implication of the dual iceberg model is that EAL learners need to continue to develop both languages to get the most advantage.

English plus – some misconceptions

Misconception 1   *'Speaking another language interferes with learning English.'*

In fact, there are various cognitive advantages to being bilingual. Research shows that bilinguals have better:

- Classification skills
- Concept formation
- Analogical reasoning
- Visual-spatial skills
- Creativity and divergent thinking
- Story-telling skills
- Language awareness

And this is apart form the obvious advantage of being able to speak more than one language!

Misconception 2   *'EAL learners should only speak English at school.'*

The dual iceberg model shows that this is not the case. On the contrary, pupils can use their first language to help them transfer knowledge to English. To get the maximum advantage they need to continue to develop both languages. (Later sections of this book provide more information on when and how to use first language to support learning.)

More misconceptions

Misconception 3 *'EAL is a special educational need.'*

Learning EAL is not a special educational need. EAL learners are no different from any other group of pupils in this respect. They have the same range of cognitive abilities. Some will have learning difficulties and disabilities; some will be gifted and talented.

Misconception 4 *'EAL learners need to learn English before they can learn with other pupils in the classroom.'*

Language is all about communication and is best learned in context. This means EAL learners need to be in the classroom where the learning is going on. They learn through listening, seeing, doing. EAL learners pick up language from their classmates through social interaction. They need to hear good models of English from native-speakers and need to be involved in active learning so they can make sense of the language.

Learning additional languages is something positive and the ability to communicate in more than one language should be valued as a great skill.

Welcome to Our Worlds

Introduction

Imagine suddenly being in another country where you don't understand the language or know the social rules and customs. You are far away from your home, family and friends......

......One of the most important things you can do for a newly arrived pupil is to create a warm, welcoming classroom environment.

This chapter gives you an idea of some of the experiences and feelings EAL learners may bring. It suggests ways that you can make sure EAL learners are included and supported by other students. You will gain some ideas about how you can reflect their cultural and linguistic identity in the physical and learning environment.

The Bullock Report (1976)

'No child should be expected to cast off the language and culture of home as he (or she) crosses the school threshold.'

A ball of confusion

For many pupils who arrive from other countries, coming to school in the UK can be very strange. The education system and schools may be organised differently. The subjects and curriculum may be very different and the style of teaching may be more (or less) formal. There could be other differences to do with culture, religious practice, society and, of course, language!

'Where I am from there were only white people. Here there are lots of black and Asian people. At first it was very strange for me.'

'I was really sad when I came here. Everything was different and I had no-one in my family with me. I missed my family and friends.'

'At school in my country the teacher talks and the pupils listen and write. I didn't really understand what to do at first when we had to work in groups.'

'In my culture we learn respect for our parents and elders. I was very shocked when I came here to see how people my age behave.'

More confusion

'In my country it is polite to look down when an adult is talking to you. In this school the teachers say look at me – it feels rude.'

'I am a Muslim and I wear a hijab to cover my head. There are no other Muslim girls from my country here. The other girls in my class made fun of me.'

'I am from a very small village. I was so surprised to come to this city with all the tall buildings and when I saw the school it was WoW! So big.'

'No-one speaks my language in my class. At first I was too embarrassed to say anything in English, so I didn't speak for the first six months.'

'People are very separate here and don't speak to each other in the street. In my country everyone is friendly. It makes me feel homesick.'

A golden hello

Learning can only take place if a pupil feels safe. So how can you help a new arrival feel welcome? Students need to feel secure and valued and that they belong:

- Don't panic! Your classroom is the best place to be for learning
- Learn how to say the pupil's name correctly. Demonstrate that their identity is important
- Don't worry if at first the pupil doesn't speak. Listening is the first step to learning a language. Encourage them to talk or respond in other ways, such as by using gestures
- Smile! and show the pupil that you are pleased they are here
- Learn how to say a few phrases in the pupil's first language. Let them see that you are making an effort as well
- Find out about the pupil's home country, religion and culture. This will help you to understand something of their world
- Teach the rest of the class how to say hello in the pupil's first language. Encourage other pupils to show the new arrival they are welcome
- Make sure you give the pupil as much of your attention as you do the other pupils. This will let them know they are as important as everyone else

Look around you

You communicate powerful messages through your classroom environment. Students need to see themselves reflected positively in their surroundings in order to feel valued and to have a sense of belonging. You can show that you value EAL learners in a number of ways:

- Put up a multilingual welcome poster on the classroom door
- Display positive images of people, objects and places from the pupil's home country
- Write signs and labels in the student's first language as well as in English
- Have dual lanquaqe books, audio books and dictionaries in the classroom
- Use stories, poetry and drama from the pupil's culture
- Celebrate religious and cultural events from the pupil's home country
- Make sure images and objects reflect the student's culture, eg foods, types of transport, housing, tools and utensils, textile designs
- Reflect the positive contribution of other cultures in all areas of the curriculum

We are family

People generally get on with people like themselves. As an educator, you have an important role in helping students to understand and respect differences and be able to get along with people who are not *'just like them'*.

Examine commonalities as well as differences so pupils can see what connects us as humans.

Generally avoid using tokenistic, negative and stereotyped images and resources. However, with older students you can use these materials to critically evaluate and deepen their understanding.

Encourage pupils to look at the differences *within* cultures as well as between them. This avoids being simplistic and stereotyping.

Challenge stereotypes and generalisations. *'Is this always the case?' 'In every situation?' 'For every person?' 'When is it not the case?' 'Where does this idea come from?'*

Respect

Respect is an important word for many pupils. It is crucially important for EAL learners that their classmates show them respect, especially when they are still in the early stages of learning English, which their peers may see negatively. You set the tone for good relationships between students from different backgrounds.

Consider how you group pupils for collaborative learning. Ensure that they have opportunities to work with different people.

Always challenge racist comments and behaviour. Show pupils that you will not tolerate it and make sure they understand why.

With paired and group activities, consider where you will place a new arrival. Select some empathetic pupils but encourage an ethos where *all* students are supportive of each other's learning.

Model the behaviours you expect from your pupils. Be explicit with them about how to show respect to others.

Hello buddy

Creating class buddies can be very supportive to EAL learners when they are new to the school. It can help to promote positive relationships between pupils from different ethnic groups. There are different models of how to organise buddies:

Model	Pros	Cons
Buddy speaks same language as EAL learner	• EAL learner can be understood and can understand more • EAL learner can feel less isolated • Can reinforce the buddy's learning	• Might negatively affect buddy's learning • Can seem as if buddy has sole responsibility
Buddy speaks English only	• Can increase understanding of different cultures • Can help EAL learner learn English	• Buddy can't translate • Buddy may be perceived as sole supporter and feel pressured
A group of buddies	• Disseminates responsibility. If one buddy is absent there are others to do the job	• Buddies may feel less personally responsible
A rotating group of buddies	• Everyone gets a chance to buddy the new arrival • EAL learner gets to know more peers	• Buddies and new pupil may not get as much time to develop friendships

What can I do for you buddy?

To be effective buddies need to be prepared for their role and clearly understand it. Some possible roles for buddies are to:

1. Encourage other pupils to be friendly and supportive.
2. Encourage the EAL learner to make friends and be more independent.
3. Be advocates who ensure that the EAL learner's concerns are heard.
4. Report back to the teacher on how well the EAL learner is doing.
5. Make sure the EAL learner is included in group work.
6. Check that the EAL learner understands the teacher's instructions.
7. Make sure the EAL learner understands any homework set.
8. Demonstrate activities to the EAL learner.

Using other languages in learning

Language is an important part of identity. For EAL learners to feel confident and have positive self-esteem, they need to feel proud of their bilingual skills and heritage. They are important resources that they can draw on in learning. However, if students do not feel that their language has a place in school, they are likely to be reluctant to use it.

EAL learners should be encouraged to use their first language:
- When they are still developing fluency in English
- To build on what they already know in their first language
- With younger pupils especially, to continue to develop their first language
- When the cognitive challenge is high
- To work through ideas
- To translate English and reinforce new words
- With pupils who share a first language
- To look at similarities and differences between English and other languages
- If they are literate in first language, to look up meanings in a bilingual dictionary

When to use English

There may be times when it is important that EAL learners use English rather than their first language. Some examples are:

- To practise English in order to improve fluency
- To rehearse orally in preparation for writing
- When learning new vocabulary in English
- When being encouraged to take risks in English to build confidence
- When preparing for a presentation in English
- When they need to practise expressing themselves quickly in English, such as exam preparation

The Ladder to Success

What to expect

Success starts with identifying the strengths and resources that an EAL learner brings. Rather than looking at what they **can't** do, look at what they **can** do and build on that. Use it to help you plan meaningful learning experiences.

In this chapter you will find tips on assessing EAL learners; the distinction between assessing language and knowledge; and getting the right balance between fluency and grammatical accuracy.

The chapter also introduces the idea of scaffolding, which you can use to help an EAL learner climb higher on the 'ladder to success'. EAL learners may be artificially restricted to the lower rungs if they are always given simplified versions of tasks. You are given some useful planning frameworks and shown a range of tools to help you build on pupils' prior knowledge, teach the language for learning and provide students with cognitive challenge.

Good practice

The ladder to success is introduced on page 36. It is a visual prompt and metaphor to help you remember the key principles in planning for EAL learners to achieve their best. However, like any ladder, it will topple if not placed on firm ground. So before working with the ladder you should be aware of the elements of good practice that firmly ground planning:

> *'It is sometimes said that what is good practice for bilingual learners is good practice for all. At one level this is a reassuring statement which suggests that teachers will not be wasting their time nor that of their monolingual pupils if they provide a learning environment which is supportive to bilinguals. But in a number of other respects it becomes a bland and uninformative truism. It has been used as an excuse for rather unspecific support which can lack either a language development focus or a curriculum development focus.'*
>
> *'Bilingual learners need both the curriculum that motivates and has relevance for them **and** the systematic language development and feedback that enables them to achieve within it.'*
>
> **Maggie Gravelle***

*Supporting Bilingual Learners in Schools, 1996 Trentham Books

Good practice – curriculum and language

What distinguishes EAL learners from their monolingual peers is that they have a double job to do:

They are learning English language and at the same time learning primarily *through* English.

As a teacher, you are responsible for teaching the concepts, skills and knowledge as well as the language needed to understand and express them. Whilst this can seem daunting, there are some simple ways in which you can integrate the two.

Remember:

Accessible and motivating Curriculm **+** Comprehensible and extending Language **=** Success for EAL Learners

Good practice – creating an inclusive classroom

The best place for an EAL learner to learn is in the classroom alongside their peers. In *Learning to Learn in a Second Language** Pauline Gibbons identifies the features of an inclusive classroom, one that is supportive for all students but especially for EAL learners:

- A positive, encouraging learning environment
- Language and learning are planned for and integrated
- Pupils are problem-solvers not information-receivers
- Planned opportunities for meaningful interaction between peers
- Many opportunities for interaction between teacher and individual pupils
- Models of language are understandable to the learner but extend their skills in expressing meaning

* Learning to Learn in a Second Language by Pauline Gibbons, Heinemann, 1993

Climbing the ladder to success

Step 2.
I know that!
Find out what learners already know. Then build confidence, fluency and accuracy.

Step 4.
Scaffolding learning
Support EAL learners to move to independence in learning.

Step 1.
Start with the positive
Find out as much as possible about your EAL learners and what they can do.

Step 3.
Planning for learning
Plan for language development and for cognitive challenge.

Step 1. Start with the positive

Initial fact-finding

Begin by finding out as much as possible about the EAL learner. Where might you find information in your school?

- Does the school have access to interpreters or anyone who speaks the pupils' first language?

- Who has a responsibility for EAL learners in the school? The Inclusion manager? EAL co-ordinator?

- What data is kept on the whole school system?
- Who is the data manger in the school?
- How can you access the data?

- Who interviews new pupils and their parents/carers?
- What information is collected? Where is it stored?

- Is there a language policy? Who would know?

- What is the target-setting process for new arrivals?
- How are they monitored?

- How is information about new pupils shared?
- What about sensitive information?

Step 1. Start with the positive

Discover what they *can* do

Next find out what the pupil can do. Some questions you could ask:

- How fluent are they in their first language?
- Can they read and write in it?
- Have they had any previous schooling?
- Have they passed any exams?
- What other achievements do they have?
- What are their skills and talents?
- What are their interests and hobbies?
- What qualities do they have that will help them learn?
- What experience do they have of English?
- Who speaks English at home?
- Who is literate in English at home?

Step 1. Start with the positive

Case study

This large London secondary school has many new arrivals. New pupils and their parents/carers are initially interviewed by the head of year and EAL co-ordinator. Background information and suggested learning strategies are shared with all staff. The pupil is assigned a buddy from the same class who introduces them to teachers, keeps an eye on them in lessons and helps them socialise in break times. A simple monitoring form is sent around with the class for the first few weeks. Teachers complete the form during the lesson to say how well the new pupil is settling into the class.

Step 1. Start with the positive

Factors to consider

Finding out what EAL learners know and can do is sometimes tricky. Are you assessing their fluency in English or their ability/potential in learning? It is important to do both, although more challenging to assess the latter.

Some factors to consider when assessing EAL learners:
* Distinguish between assessing English language acquisition and grasp of concepts and knowledge
* Take into account how long the pupil has been learning English
* Consider how cultural conventions about behaviours, gender roles or respect may influence the way a pupil responds
* Be aware that often levels in the different language skills of listening, speaking, reading and writing may vary
* Giving a formal assessment is likely to mask a pupil's true potential
* Assess in ways and contexts that are age and culture appropriate
* Be alert to cultural bias in assessments, especially in reading
* Use methods of assessment that do not rely solely on responses in English or in writing

Step 1. Start with the positive

Tips

- Using observational assessment you are likely to see a greater range of communication skills
- Setting tasks where pupils respond non-verbally can allow them to demonstrate knowledge, skills and understanding
- Using 'yes or no' questions or offering alternative answers/multiple choice can take away the pressure of having to formulate complex answers
- Use visuals to support understanding
- Take opportunities to assess pupils using first language wherever possible
- Using assessment information from ordinary everyday classroom activities can be less stressful for pupils
- A teaching assistant can be an extra pair of eyes and ears to collect assessment evidence
- Use a wide range of assessment sources to build a full picture of the pupil

Note: If you are using assessment data to place EAL learners in sets, it is strongly advised that they are placed according to their potential, not their current English language fluency.

Step 2. I know that!

Making connections

Learning happens when we can 'hook' new ideas on to what we already know. If learning does not connect with what is already known it will soon be forgotten.

This is particularly important for EAL learners. They need to make connections between new learning in English and knowledge gained from a different culture and through another language.

You may have experienced trying to read a novel from an unfamiliar cultural context and finding it difficult. The names, locations, references, activities felt alien and hard to imagine or fathom. For EAL learners the same cultural unfamiliarity in the classroom can be a barrier to learning.

You can help EAL learners by considering what kinds of previous knowledge and experience they may have. Think about what elements from their home language and culture you can bring to your lessons and include things from their experience to make the learning more culturally familiar.

Step 2. I know that!

Tools to find out what learners know

The tools below can be used to find out:

- What pupils already know about a particular topic

- What gaps there are in their knowledge

- What misconceptions pupils have about the topic

You will find a description of each tool in the following pages.

Step 2. I know that!

Brainstorming

Brainstorming is an informal group activity where members are given a topic, often a single word, and then spontaneously share information and generate or develop ideas around the subject with one person recording what is said in writing. It is a simple but effective collaborative tool, often useful at the beginning of a new topic.

Brainstorming opens up and values ideas from a range of cultures and backgrounds. It enables EAL learners to have some familiarity with the vocabulary of the topic. The images and ideas that are associated with words are culturally specific and will vary from individual to individual. As well as giving you a picture of what pupils know, it can also give you some insight into their world.

> **Example**
>
> A year 7 class studying Macbeth in English was looking at imagery associated with sleep. Pupils worked in small groups to list as many words to do with sleep as possible. The teacher placed the one EAL leaner new to English with a supportive group. Groups had then to classify their words as positive, negative or neutral. This allowed the EAL learner to contribute ideas and learn new vocabulary. She was able to participate with her peers in the lesson.

Step 2. I know that!

KWL grids

KWL grids are a great way of tapping into pupils' knowledge and of identifying misconceptions that can be addressed later in your teaching. They also enable pupils to ask their own questions so you can build on their interests and personalise learning.

KWL stands for:
- What I already **K**now
- What I **W**ant to find out
- What I have **L**earnt

TOPIC:		
What I already know	What I want to find out	What I have learnt

1. In column one pupils record their ideas. If you nominate one pupil to do this it frees an EAL learner to focus on articulating their ideas. They can also draw to represent what they know.
2. In column two pupils formulate questions that they want to investigate. Working as a team helps an EAL learner to construct questions.
3. Pupils fill in column three after they have done activities to investigate the topic. It is a good way for pupils to see the connections between their first ideas and new learning.

Step 2. I know that!

KWL grids – an example

Example

A year 5 class with 2 EAL new arrivals was beginning a cross-curricular Drama/Citizenship project about refugees.

Pupils shared what they knew with a talk partner. The new arrivals were partnered with fluent English speakers who could help explain ideas and enable EAL learners to articulate their own ideas.

Pairs joined to make groups of four, pooled ideas and thought about what questions they wanted answers to. One EAL learner had a lot of knowledge to bring to this topic, which enhanced her self-esteem.

At the end of the project pupils reflected on their initial ideas and questions and on what they had learned.

Before I thought …

Now I know

I didn't know that …

Step 2. I know that!

Concept cartoons

There are full details of concept cartoons at www.conceptcartoons.com. First developed in Science to provoke discussion and stimulate thinking, they depict an abstract idea in an everyday situation, thus making it concrete and more accessible. Cartoon-style characters consider an idea and give alternative interpretations, only one of which is acceptable. This allows pupils to position themselves with one interpretation or discard some alternatives.

There is plenty of scope for developing your own cartoons. Some teachers, instead of using cartoon characters, have used photographs of themselves with accompanying speech bubbles.

There's a hole in the cloud and the rain falls out

Clouds bump into each other and shake the rain out

Rain falls when the land gets too dry

Drops of water join together and get heavy and fall

Rains comes from clouds sweating

Step 2. I know that!

How to use concept cartoons

Concept cartoons are good tools for informally assessing EAL learners' knowledge in that they represent an idea visually and have minimal text. Even if students cannot fully express their thinking, you get a good indication of their understanding. They work well as an introduction to a topic, at the end to assess understanding, or later as revision. Use them as group activities so that pupils have the opportunity to hear and respond to alternative interpretations.

Example

A year 3 class with several EAL learners in the early stages of English fluency were investigating what plants need to grow. They had looked at different plants, drawn them and learned the names of different parts. Before doing some practical investigations, they looked at a concept cartoon showing a plant in a dark cupboard. All pupils were stimulated by the discussion. The EAL learners were able to hear language modelled by their peers and expressed their opinions. The teacher used careful questioning and prompting to draw out the pupils' different views and their reasoning.

Step 2. I know that!

Confidence, fluency and accuracy

There is a fine balance between encouraging an EAL learner to communicate orally in English and teaching them how to use English accurately. Too much correction of language may inhibit a learner from experimenting and trying out new language. In the first instance, it is more important that their communication is understood. There are sensitive ways of correcting students' errors and giving them good models of spoken English (see Let's Talk About It, pages 70 – 80).

1. Silent period
It is common for a new arrival to go through a 'silent period'. They will still be listening, trying to make sense of the language around them and learning.

* You can use non-verbal responses to check their understanding, such as a show of hands

* You could give all pupils a set of 'traffic light cards' which they can place on the table: Green = OK, I understand   Amber = a bit unsure   Red = help!

* You might get a pupil to demonstrate their understanding by asking them to follow instructions

Step 2. I know that!

Confidence, fluency and accuracy

2. Building confidence and fluency
- Build confidence by showing patience when pupils struggle to find the right words
- Allow time to form answers and use strategies such as 'think-pair-share'
- Praise learners for taking risks and trying, even if they make errors

3. Building accuracy
- Give pupils lots of opportunity to hear good spoken models from adults and peers
- *Recasting* is a very powerful and positive way of providing correct versions of language (see page 72)
- Plan opportunities for pupils to rehearse and report back from team activities. A student new to English could practise and say just one or two sentences

Step 3. Planning for learning

Two challenges

EAL learners are as able as any other pupils; they just haven't yet become fluent in English. There are two big challenges for you:

1. **Planning for cognitive challenge**
   To make the curriculum accessible for EAL learners without 'dumbing down' the learning.

2. **Planning for language development**
   To make language comprehensible and also improve pupils' language for learning skills.

The diagram on the next page is a useful tool for planning activities that will develop the thinking and skills of EAL learners. In turn, this will demand more complex language to express ideas. Planning for EAL learners should move from concrete experience to abstract: from A to B to C. Activities in D are both undemanding and abstract. They include activities such as copying or mindless repeating without understanding where there is little, if any, learning potential.

Step 3. Planning for learning

A planning frame

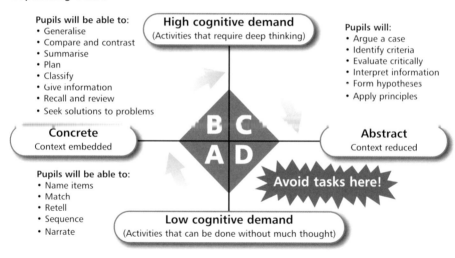

Pupils will be able to:
- Generalise
- Compare and contrast
- Summarise
- Plan
- Classify
- Give information
- Recall and review
- Seek solutions to problems

High cognitive demand
(Activities that require deep thinking)

Pupils will:
- Argue a case
- Identify criteria
- Evaluate critically
- Interpret information
- Form hypotheses
- Apply principles

Concrete
Context embedded

B C
A D

Abstract
Context reduced

Pupils will be able to:
- Name items
- Match
- Retell
- Sequence
- Narrate

Avoid tasks here!

Low cognitive demand
(Activities that can be done without much thought)

Step 3. Planning for learning

Planning in action

The example below demonstrates how to plan activities that increase in challenge and are accessible to EAL learners in context.

Example

 A Pupils work with a partner to match pictures of animals and their names. EAL learners can say what the name is in their first language, if they know. Those who can write in their first language could write the names.

 B Pupils work together to group the animals in a way that makes sense to them. You should not influence their choices. The aim is to find out what they know and to uncover their thinking. You create a purpose for communication.

 C Pupils group the animals and then explain how they have classified them. You could scaffold this by drawing on their first language, using careful questioning or providing labels with suggested criteria.

What could this look like in *your* lessons?

Step 3. Planning for learning

Planning for language development

When planning for learning you need to consider what language students will need to know in order to be successful. This includes more than the key vocabulary. Vocabulary is a starting point but EAL learners will need whole structures to be able to communicate effectively.

Think about what language functions pupils will need to perform, eg analysing, explaining, evaluating, comparing. What phrases will they need to be able to do that? The example below demonstrates planning for language development in Maths:

Topic: SHAPES				
Learning objectives	**Activities**	**Language functions**	**Language structure**	**Vocabulary**
Describe, measure and compare shapes using mathematical language	Classifying shapes Barrier game	Describing Comparing	It has/they have It is/they are They are They both.. Both ... and ... The same/ different	Square/rectangle/triangle circle/ diamond Line – straight/curved/parallel Angle Equal

Step 4. Scaffolding learning

Scaffolding in this context is a metaphor based on the ideas of Vygotsky. It represents how, working with more expert others, a pupil can achieve something beyond what they can do alone. (Think of how parents seem intuitively to know the right amount of support to give their children.)

A scaffold is a temporary structure. It is put in place as support for a learner to access higher levels. Gradually, the learner takes over more of the control until they are independent. They are then ready for a new scaffold to take them to the next level. Learning is a continuous movement from dependence to independence.

EAL learners need the language for learning to be carefully scaffolded so they can express what they know through English and continue to develop their academic language skills. The role of the teacher and collaboration with other pupils are key components of scaffolding for EAL learners. They both provide good models of language. The language of peers can be closer to where an EAL learner is and therefore a valuable stepping stone to developing fluency.

Step 4. Scaffolding learning

In the remaining pages of this Pocketbook you will find a range of tools to help you scaffold learning for EAL learners. The next five chapters cover the following five areas:

1. Visual support.

2. Recasting, talk frames and spoken models.

3. Building vocabulary.

4. Active reading.

5. Models and modelling.

Collaborative learning is a thread through ALL chapters.

Extra, Extra

 Welcome to Our Worlds

 The Ladder to Success

 I See What You Mean

 Let's Talk About It

 What's in a Word?

 Reading Between the Lines

 Get it Write!

I See What You Mean

Using visuals

Using visuals enables EAL learners to start from a concrete experience. This can be a powerful way of triggering students' memory and interest and of making learning fun for all pupils.

Pictures, objects, photos, diagrams, maps, graphs, drawings, paintings, video, mime and demonstration are all great ways of providing visual support for understanding and helping EAL learners to develop their use of English in context. You can help EAL learners make sense of the lesson content actively by using these as much as possible.

Good use of the internet, interactive whiteboards, digital cameras and digital video cameras will extend visual support. If you are looking for an image of something in particular, simply typing your search into Google and selecting 'images' will uncover a huge bank to choose from.

In this chapter you will find a range of visual tools.

Picture this!

Photographs, pictures, drawings and paintings can be great starting points for EAL learners. Working in pairs or small groups, students study the visual stimulus and answer questions that require thought and discussion and that open up a subject, idea or situation:

Where are they?

What can you see?

What year is it?

What are they saying?

Describe the people.

Do you think they are rich or poor?

What does it remind you of?

What are they doing?

Asking questions of a picture

You can divide the questions into three stages to help scaffold learning for EAL learners:

1 **Describe**

Ask pupils to begin by describing in detail what they can see. This is helpful to an EAL learner because it starts with the concrete and familiarises them with relevant vocabulary.

2 **Explain**

Next ask them to talk about their ideas. *What is happening? Are there any people? What are they doing? How old do they look? What is their relationship? What makes you think so?*

Ask them to use words to describe the feelings of the image, eg: *happy, sad, dark, light, warm, cold.* Or abstract ideas: *loyalty, honesty, danger, love, safety.* What in the image makes them say that?

3 **Infer**

Ask them to think about where the image is from. *Who made it? Who for? Why? Where is it from? What is the image not showing you? What has been left out? What would you expect to see just outside of the picture?*

Sequencing

You can ask pupils to work in small groups or pairs to sequence images. The images could be part of a narrative, a chronology of events, a timeline or a process. An EAL learner with little English is able to develop and demonstrate their conceptual understanding in this kind of activity.

Some examples:

- A fictional story, comic strip, poem, film sequence or play
- Real events – a story from the news, an historical account
- A process, such as how volcanoes are formed, the life cycle of a frog, recycling cans
- A timeline showing how telephones have changed in design over decades
- Following a sequence – stages in problem-solving, a recipe, making paper

The Mystery Object

The Mystery Object is another tool to stimulate thinking and discussion. You could use a real object, an image of an everyday object taken from an unusual angle or an image of a partially obscured object. Pupils can hypothesise what they think it is, who might use it, where it is from.

Taking a real object, you might start with using the senses to explore it.

What does it look like?

Can you taste it?
What does it taste like?

What does it feel like?

Does it have a smell?
What does it smell like?

Does it make a noise?
What does it sound like?

Spot the difference

It is often easier to see something if you have a point of comparison. Looking at and comparing images can help make characteristics more obvious to EAL learners. Generally, this generates most discussion if you select highly contrasting images. For example:

1. A selection of photos showing two contrasting places, eg two countries or a rural and urban environment; photos of the same place but at different times, eg time of day, season, in the past and present.

2. Images showing positive and negative views of the same subject, eg an idealised, romantic painting of poor Victorian children and a painting showing a harsher, grimier depiction.

3. Pictures showing the same or similar activities from different cultures, eg everyday life, religious worship, sports.

Spot the difference 2

4. Comparing graphical information, eg two different approaches to finding mathematical solutions; graphs showing the same information but with different results.

5. Pictures showing objects with some similar and some different features, eg percussion instruments; stringed musical instruments from different cultures.

6. Pictures showing contrasting actions, eg children behaving in a safe/dangerous way; alternative ways of dealing with situations; alternative story endings.

Moving image

Moving image can literally bring something to life and is an excellent way of supporting understanding for EAL learners. However, there are pitfalls. Below are some typical difficulties an EAL learner may experience with film/video and ways you might overcome them:

BARRIER	SOLUTION
Too much information. EAL learner does not know what is relevant and what is not.	Give the student a precise focus for viewing, such as one clear question. Or ask them to count the instances of something happening.
Difficulty in understanding new information.	Start with prediction activities. Students will make more sense of what they see if they activate prior knowledge.
Difficulty in concentrating for long periods of time.	Limit the length of sequences, say to a maximum of 20 minutes.
It is hard for an EAL learner to watch, listen, process information and take notes at the same time.	Limit note-taking – use other strategies such as ticking, numbering, sequencing, or wait until after viewing to make notes.

Tools to exploit moving image

There are many creative ways of using video. Below are just a few that have proven to be successful. No doubt you can think of many more!

Prediction
Show a still image from the video or the first few seconds of the clip. Ask pupils to discuss:
* *What do you think the clip will be about?*
* *What else will you see?*
* *What else will you hear?*

Quick draw
Ask pupils to draw as a response to what they see. Give a time limit to help them work speedily!

No sound
Play the video with muted sound. Ask pupils to work in teams to create the voiceover or dialogue for the video. This enables EAL learners to develop language in context. You can even ask them to do a bilingual version. Students could role play or read their scripts in sync. with the video when they have finished.

Concept maps

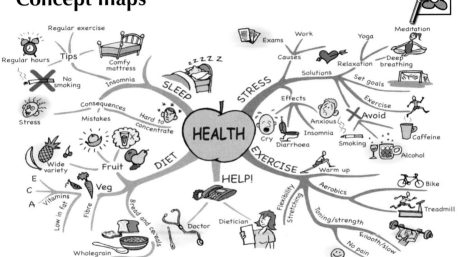

Concept maps are useful for generating discussion. They show how pupils are thinking and linking ideas, provide information to help you plan for learning, and help EAL learners to see the big picture.

Concept maps – how to do it

1. Organise pupils into teams. Give each team a large sheet of paper and ask them to write the topic in the centre.

2. You could start by brainstorming what pupils know about the topic first. Ask them to record each piece of information (or drawing) on a separate card or post-it. This allows pupils to manipulate ideas when they create their maps.

3. This tool will work best if you model it first with a different topic. Think aloud while you group ideas together; write or draw them; connect them with lines and write along the connecting lines. Use different colours to group closely linked ideas.

4. You could show pupils a range of differently styled concept maps to inspire their creativity.

5. Give each team colour pens to construct their maps.

Example

Each team of three in a Y9 Geography revision lesson was given sets of blank cards, blu-tac, colour pens and a large piece of paper. They wrote the topic **Inequality** in the centre of the paper. On the cards they wrote key words and drew pictures or symbols to represent these. They arranged the cards on the paper and drew lines to connect related elements. A set of key vocabulary and picture 'help' cards was available and pupils could choose whether to use them. There were four EAL learners in the class and two of them chose to use the cards.

Let's Talk
About It

The importance of talk for learning

A classroom with plenty of opportunities for speaking and listening is very supportive to EAL learners. They need to develop social talk in English to form relationships with peers. They also need to develop spoken English for learning as well as continuing to improve their first language. Pupils learn through talk by developing, testing out and revising ideas. This is an important foundation for reading and writing (see last two sections of this book).

Listening to and communicating with fluent speakers is a key means of learning English. Different subjects will give opportunities for different kinds of talk.

For effective 'talk for learning' you should:
- Plan opportunities for structured talk
- Be clear about the purposes and audiences of talk
- Provide models of talk
- Scaffold talk with prompts or 'talk frames'
- Build in time for reflection

In the following pages you will find a range of tools for scaffolding speaking and listening.

Teacher scaffolding – explaining

EAL learners develop language by first hearing it in a meaningful context. Making what you say humorous and interesting will also capture all pupils' attention! There are various ways in which you can help an EAL learner to understand your explanations:

Use of visuals
Use props, puppets and images to support what you say.
(See previous chapter.)

Repetition
Repeat key words and important phrases.

Rephrasing
Offer an explanation using more complex language and then rephrase using simpler language.

Keywords
Display key vocabulary and point, circle or highlight as you speak. (See following chapter.)

Body language
Use mime, gesture, facial expressions, acting out, pointing.

Demonstration
Show pupils what you mean by demonstrating. Explain as you demonstrate so the meaning of your words is clear.

Teacher scaffolding – recasting

Recasting is something that parents do naturally with their children. It is a positive way of correcting an EAL learner's English. It also enables you to model how to extend their English and thinking. In recasting you respond to a pupil by providing a grammatically correct or longer version of what the pupil has said. Here are some examples:

'It go under water.'

'Yes, the weight **went** under the water. It **sank**. Why do you think it sank?'

'Music very fast.'

'Yes, the music **is** fast. The **tempo** is fast.'

'William he got good soldiers ... he win.'

'Ah, so you think William **won** because he had **better** soldiers... a **stronger army**?'

Teacher scaffolding – questioning

No hands rule
Instead of the convention of asking students to put their hands up to answer questions and then choosing from those who raise their hands, you can train them to follow the 'no hands rule'. Explain that when you ask a question you will choose named pupils to answer. This allows you to frame questions to match particular learners. It's a good strategy for making sure that you include all members of the class in answering questions.

Yes or no questions
Asking 'yes' or 'no' questions is a good way of checking understanding if a learner has limited English.

Multiple choice questions
Giving a pupil the answers in the form of multiple choice provides them with the language they need to respond, eg *'Is the line curved, straight or wavy?'*

Traffic lights
You can get all pupils to respond non-verbally by showing you a thumbs up, thumbs down or thumbs in the middle for *'yes'*, *'no'*, *'not sure'*. Or you could give them green, red and amber cards to hold up to signal the same.

Teacher scaffolding – modelling

Modelling oral language is a key way of scaffolding learning for EAL learners. They can hear appropriate language used in context. Either you can model the language, or pupils who are fluent in English can provide models in collaborative activities. Alternatively, you could use DVDs showing 'experts'. In this case you will need to explicitly draw attention to the language used.

Some suggestions of oral language you might model:
- Telling a story
- Giving instructions
- Describing an object, person or place
- Explaining how to make or do something
- Recounting an event, or steps in a process
- Presenting two sides of an argument
- Describing and interpreting a piece of art or music
- Evaluating a product or performance
- Persuading someone of a point of view

Talk partners

Pairing students as 'talk partners' is a good way of helping EAL learners in that it allows them time to process information and formulate a response with support from a peer. You then pose a question or problem and give pupils a defined amount of time, say 30 seconds or two minutes, to discuss with their talk partner and come up with an answer.

Advantages of using talk partners:
- It takes the pressure away from being put on the spot
- It prevents the 'rabbit caught in the headlights' brain freeze
- It overcomes the fear of giving 'the wrong answer'
- It stops '*I don't know*'
- Students are prepared to take more risks
- Much richer responses are generated
- All pupils get the chance to talk
- Pupils get a chance to test out ideas
- It's a very simple tool to use

Talk frames and prompts

Talk frames and prompts provide the language EAL learners need to structure their talk. You can create frames that give pupils the sequence for talk, as in examples A and B, or you can offer a menu to choose from, as in example C opposite. Frames and prompts such as these can also be used to scaffold writing (see final chapter).

A. Drama, PE, Music

Evaluating my Performance

- What I did well was …
- I showed this by …
- I need to improve …
- I will do this by …
- I will know I am successful because…

B. Science

Report back on an Investigation

- Our hypothesis
- Equipment we used
- What we did
- How we did it
- What we found out
- What our results show

Talk frames and prompts

C. English, Humanities, Science, PSHE, Citizenship

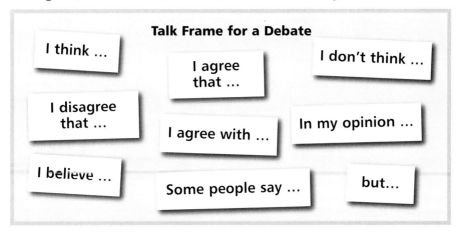

Talk Frame for a Debate

I think …

I agree that …

I don't think …

I disagree that …

I agree with …

In my opinion …

I believe …

Some people say …

but…

Barrier games

Barrier games involve giving and receiving instructions and information where there is a physical barrier so pupils can't see the work being discussed on the other side. They require students to be very precise and explicit in their use of language.

Two examples
Ask pupils to sit opposite each other and place a barrier, such as a large book, between them. Or they could sit back-to-back:

1. Give both students a copy of the same map but marked with different routes. Student A describes their route to student B and student B marks it out on their map. They then swap roles. At the end they can compare their maps to see if the routes match. Pupils can evaluate how clear and full their instructions were.

2. Students have a set of construction materials or shapes. Student A makes a model or pattern and instructs student B so they can replicate it. They can then check

More barrier games

Barrier games are very adaptable and can be used to help EAL learners to learn and practise a range of language. The more they practise, the better they become. Other examples of where barrier games could be used include:

- Role-playing a telephone conversation
- Describing a drawing or picture
- Spotting differences
- Describing positions, relationships between objects, shapes
- Sequencing pictures or diagrams
- Completing unfinished diagrams
- Labelling pictures or photos
- Drawing pictures or diagrams
- Making models using clay, card, molecule models or recycled materials
- Matching words and pictures
- Matching descriptions and people, places or objects
- Describing locations on a map

Role play and drama tools

Role play and drama tools are effective for the development of language because they allow for experiential learning. There is a huge range of drama tools that can be used creatively in all areas of the curriculum. It is beyond the scope of this book to go into great detail (see the *Drama for Learning Pocketbook* for a wealth of material), but some ideas include:

- Acting out stories, poems and plays
- Debating an issue
- An imaginary dinner party with fictional, real or historical characters
- Interviews
- Role-playing '*The Culture Show*' or '*The Book Programme*'
- 'Hot seating' a character
- 'Freeze framing' a scene and speaking the thoughts of the characters
- Role-playing an 'expert' such as a scientist, historian, musician or art critic

What's in a Word?

Building vocabulary

Vocabulary is best taught in the context of learning and while pupils are engaged in meaningful activities. This supports EAL learners' **understanding** of words. Make sure you emphasise keywords and repeat them. EAL learners will need lots of opportunities to **practise** speaking the words. Encourage them to use new words.

They will also need to **revisit** and **revise** key vocabulary. Starter and plenary activities and games provide excellent opportunities for this and also make learning fun for all pupils.

Glossaries, word mats (ie laminated table mats of words, often with supporting visuals) and displays are all helpful supports for learning new vocabulary.

In this chapter you will find a variety of tools to introduce, use, extend and revisit vocabulary. You can use them to help EAL learners to learn the key words of the curriculum or your subject.

Basic word grammar

Whatever your subject specialism, it is useful to know the basic word categories and what they do. This will help you to support EAL learners to learn English in your classroom.

Noun	This is a thing. It can be a concrete thing like a *book* or *Africa*, or an abstract thing like *love*.
Verb	This is a word that describes an action like *run*, a mental process like *think*, or a state like *be*.
Determiner	This word goes in front of a noun to say which noun it is, for example *a* shoe, *that* car, *those* people, *my* opinion.
Adjective	This word gives you more information about a noun, for instance a *great* idea, *Turkish* food, *brown* eyes.
Adverb	This word gives you more information about a verb, for instance walk *slowly*, think *carefully*, shine *brightly*.
Connective	This word joins sentences or phrases together, for example *and*, *but*, *however*.

Display

Create a language-rich environment by displaying keywords and supporting visuals. You can make sure they don't become just wallpaper by referring to them in lessons and regularly changing displays to support the topics being learned. This also maintains pupils' interest!

You can help EAL learners to engage with vocabulary by removing the labels and asking students to place them correctly. You could also label equipment and areas of the classroom including bilingual labels.

Lexical sets

EAL learners will find it easier to learn groups of associated words rather than random groups. These can be displayed, made into glossaries for pupils to keep, or laminated and used as word mats for use in writing or speaking.

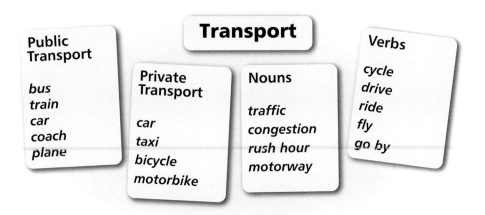

Transport

Public Transport

bus
train
car
coach
plane

Private Transport

car
taxi
bicycle
motorbike

Nouns

traffic
congestion
rush hour
motorway

Verbs

cycle
drive
ride
fly
go by

Word roots

Many English words come from Latin and Greek. It is helpful to EAL learners (and all learners!) to point out the connections between words from the same root. Seeing the patterns aids students' understanding and helps them to remember and recall words.

triangle

tripod

tri = *from Greek meaning 'three'*

triple

trio

triplet

Learning and using word families

It makes sense to teach together the word families that contain vocabulary pupils are likely to need. It is also useful to indicate the word category (noun, verb, etc) as this gives a clue as to how to use it. For example:

Often EAL learners struggle to put new words into sentences. You can model this for them:

- You can use a **calculator** for this problem
- I used **calculation** to solve the problem
- Can you **calculate** this sum?
- We **calculated** the distance between A and B

Flashcards

Flashcards are picture cards. It's a good idea to
create sets of flashcards for different topics,
showing images that illustrate key vocabulary
and ideas. Flashcards are great tools for
memorising information. Create A4 cards
to use with the whole class and for display
or smaller cards for groups and individuals.

Suggestions for using flashcards:
* To support meaning when you are explaining and questioning
* To help pupils peer assess each other on vocabulary in pairs
* To assess the EAL learner on how well they have remembered new words
* Give them to the EAL learner, after the introduction, to refer to during the lesson
* You can adjust the number of flashcards and vocabulary items to be learned
  according to the pupil
* More fluent pupils can explain the meaning of the vocabulary
* You could put the word on the back

Matching

Matching word and picture cards helps EAL learners to recognise words by sight and associate them with their meaning. You can also make matching word and definition cards. Creating such cards can be a good time investment as they are a versatile resource. They can be used to:

1. Introduce or remember key words
perhaps at the start of a lesson to activate prior knowledge/recap an earlier lesson, or as a plenary activity to assess learning.

2. Revise key words
Pupils can test each other by showing a picture and asking their partner to select the correct label. Or they can show the label and ask their partner to find the picture. They can then turn over the labels and see if their partner can remember the words.

Matching games

You can use matching word and picture cards to play games. Here are a couple of ideas, but you can invent your own!

Snap

Pupils play in pairs. They should divide the cards into two equal piles and place them face down. Player one turns their top card face up in the centre of the table. Player two turns over their top card and places it on top of the first. They continue until they see a matching pair. The first player to call out the word keeps all of the cards in the pile. The player with the most cards wins.

The Memory Game

Pupils play in small groups. They place all the cards face down and spread them out on the table. The first player turns over two cards. If it's a matching pair they say the word, keep the cards and have a second go. If not they turn the cards face down again. Then the next player goes and so on. The player with the most cards wins.

For speed, print the words and pictures cards in contrasting colours.

Odd-one-out

Odd-one-out can be used with words, symbols or pictures. It's a way of getting pupils to think about words or ideas, their qualities and possible similarities and differences. It can be a challenging cognitive activity that is also accessible for EAL learners with little English.

1. Create sets of three or four words or pictures.
2. Ask pupils to say which is the odd one out and why.
3. It is more challenging if there are several possible answers.
4. Tell them you are interested in their reasons.

sea **river** **canal**

Sea is the odd one out because it only has 3 letters! Canal and river both have 5 letters.

Canal is the odd one out because sea and river are natural features but canal is made by humans.

Sea is the odd one out because river and canal both flow in one direction. Sea is a body of water.

Word banks

Word banks help EAL learners to broaden their vocabulary. You can create word banks for pupils to use as oral prompts in lessons. Or you could store them on computer where students can access them for writing.

Suggestions for using word banks:

- Copy them on to laminated cards and place them on tables so pupils can use them in the lesson

- Create differentiated word banks to stretch pupils at all levels

- Make sure EAL learners know how to say all the words in their bank and that they understand the meanings

'Alternatives to say' word bank

Washing lines

Often EAL learners have difficulty with nuance. The washing line tool can be used with words that describe different degrees or strengths and that can be sequenced on a continuum. It is used to extend EAL learners' vocabulary range and helps students to be precise and accurate with language.

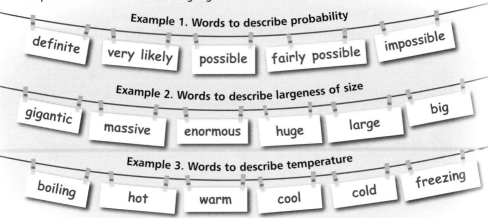

Example 1. Words to describe probability

definite | very likely | possible | fairly possible | impossible

Example 2. Words to describe largeness of size

gigantic | massive | enormous | huge | large | big

Example 3. Words to describe temperature

boiling | hot | warm | cool | cold | freezing

Washing lines – how to do it

Print out the sequence of words on to separate A4 cards and make one set per team.

1. Organise pupils into teams and give each pupil a different word card.
2. Team members stand in a line in the correct order, each pupil holding up their word card.
3. Teams check to see if there are any differences in the way they have each ordered their words.
4. Allow them to swap places and explain any changes.

You can display the 'washing line' by pegging the words on to a string. This allows you and the pupils to refer back to them.

Reading Between the Lines

What is reading?

Reading is a search for meaning. A reader has to be active and has to think to reconstruct a writer's message. To make sense of print the reader needs to have four types of knowledge:

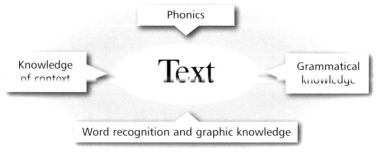

Phonic knowledge	– the sounds in a language	
Graphic knowledge	– the written representations of sounds	
Grammar	– the language system	
Context	– knowledge of the world, the culture and topic	

Difficulties EAL learners may have with reading

Phonics and graphic knowledge
- Difficulty decoding words
- May be unfamiliar with Roman script

Word recognition
- Do not understand the vocabulary
- Confused by words with multiple meanings

Grammar
- Unfamiliar with patterns that help to make meaning
- Do not understand idiomatic language, metaphor, irony

Knowledge of context
- No background knowledge of content
- Content culturally unfamiliar

Reading for meaning

Because EAL learners can often decode words they do not understand, it is particularly important to focus on reading for meaning. EAL learners may not realise that they need to self-monitor and question what they are reading. They need to actively engage with the text to make meaning.

How you can help:
- Consider what cultural knowledge is needed to understand texts you use
- Select texts from the EAL learner's cultural background when possible
- Make explicit reference to idiomatic language (eg *it's raining cats and dogs*)
- Encourage EAL learners to guess the meaning of words from the context
- Teach vocabulary
- Encourage readers to ask their own 'why' questions of a text
- Model the behaviours of a good reader

In this section the focus is on tools to help EAL learners read to learn.

A reading environment

Have a range of books and texts available in your classroom to support learning. You can use these as resources for independent, individual and small group activities.

Topic book boxes
Collect a range of books and texts about the topics you teach. Select a range of simple and more challenging texts. Include texts with lots of visuals.

Bilingual books and books in other languages
These can enhance an EAL learner's understanding and support the continued development of first language.

Simplified versions of texts
Where available, these can sometimes be a useful introduction for an EAL learner to complex whole class texts.

Dictionaries
Have a range of dictionaries available for older pupils to use including:
- General dictionaries
- Bilingual dictionaries
- Subject dictionaries
- Picture dictionaries

Audio books
Audio books can support the development of independent reading.

Mind the GAPS – questions to ask about a text

Asking GAPS questions is an excellent way to help EAL learners to understand the wider context and to use this knowledge in reading a text.

GAPS Questions

G   **Genre: What kind of text is it?**
Eg biography, instructional, email, memo, study guide, joke

A   **Audience: Who is it written for?**
Eg teenagers, women, teachers, parents of young children

P   **Purpose: Why is it written?**
Eg to persuade, entertain, frighten, make someone laugh

S   **Source: Where would you find it?**
Eg in a newspaper, text book, diary, on a cereal box

Why am I reading this? What do I want to know?

We read for a purpose. It could be for pleasure, to find out the latest celebrity gossip, to study for an exam, to find out train times, etc. The way we read depends on our purpose. EAL learners need to practise reading in all curriculum areas and to experience a wide range of texts.

You can help EAL learners by being clear about the purpose for reading and ensuring they know what kind of reading best suits the purpose. You could model skimming, scanning and close reading.

Strategy	Purpose	Example
Skim	Reading to get an overall impression or big picture.	Reading a newspaper, reading around a subject, browsing on the internet.
Scan	Reading for specific information.	Locating a route on a map, selecting a TV programme from a listings guide, looking up a phone number in a directory.
Close	Reading for all the details.	Studying for an exam, following a recipe or set of instructions, reading a novel.

Before, during and after reading

EAL learners need help to make sense of text and to develop good reading strategies. Before, during and after reading tools help them to do both. Here are some suggestions:

Before
To help students to activate prior knowledge and anticipate the content of the text, seeing the big picture:

- Brainstorm what they already know about the topic
- You tell pupils the title; they predict 10 words that will be in the text
- Give pupils 5 –10 words or quotations from the text. They suggest a title
- Use images from or linked to the text for prediction
- Use music or sound related to the text to stimulate ideas
- Show the first line or paragraph. Ask pupils to guess what comes next
- Give pupils a list of statements about the content of the text to discuss

Before, during and after reading

During
To help students understand the purpose for reading and to read for meaning:
* Give pupils a focus question or ask GAPS questions (see page 100)
* Provide opportunities to skim, scan, close read
* Use paired reading
* Give pupils a list of true or false statements to respond to (see next page)
* Pause at significant points and predict what comes next
* Use text reconstruction activities, eg sequencing and jigsaw reading (see pages 105-106)
* Use text-marking activities such as highlighting, numbering, labelling (see page 108)

After
To help students reflect, draw conclusions or evaluate their reading, ask them to:
* Summarise, eg pupils suggest a title for each paragraph
* Use cloze activities, ie fill in parts of the text you have removed
* Transfer information to a different format such as a graph or diagram
* Write an alternative ending, give an opposing point of view
* Make a visual response – eg draw a concept map or timeline
* Role play

True or false?

True or false statements help pupils to focus on reading to understand. In the example below pupils say what they think before reading. Then they read to confirm what they think, find out something they don't know, or correct a misconception.

Global Warming		
T= True, F=False, ?= don't know	before	after
1 *The Earth is getting warmer.*	T	T
2 *Cows cause global warming.*	?	?
3 *There is nothing I can do about global warming.*	T	F

- You can design 'True or False' with varying levels of challenge. Students have to find literal, inferential or evaluative meaning
- You could create a *Prove it!* column where pupils record evidence from the text
- You might include statements for which there is no evidence in the text

Sequencing

Having to sequence cut-up text requires pupils to read for meaning. They have to make sense of what they are reading to be able to complete the task successfully.

- You can take any continuous written text, copy it onto card and cut it up
- You can vary the level of challenge depending on where you cut the text
- The text can contain visuals as well as words

> Religion was very important in the Middle Ages. People thought God controlled every part of their lives. Every village had a church.

> This was usually in the middle of the village. Everybody had to go to church on Sundays and other holy days. The church had special services for birth, marriage and death.

> One way they learned about the life and teachings of Christ was from paintings on the walls of the church.

A word of caution – test out the activity first. You need to make sure you have made the breaks at boundaries where it is possible to deduct the logical order.

Jigsaw reading

Jigsaw reading is an excellent example of a sequencing activity where pupils collaborate to reconstruct text.

Preparation:

1. Decide on the size of groups (4-6) and select the text to be used.
2. Cut the text into enough sections to allow each member of the group one section.
3. You can make some sections easier to read and match to students' needs.
4. Copy onto card – one set per group.

Each person in turn should read their piece aloud and describe any visuals. The aim for the group is to read, listen, discuss and agree the correct sequence.

THE ONE IMPORTANT RULE!

The group must complete the task without looking at each other's cards. They may need to ask fellow group members to re-read sections in order to come to a consensus.

Who? What? When? Where? Why?

Asking the key questions *Who? What? When? Where? Why?* helps EAL learners to understand the gist or the BIG picture. It is important they have this context before reading a text more closely for information.

This tool works well with fiction and recounts such as newspaper stories and historical events.

You could ask pupils to highlight parts of the text that give the answers to the questions. (See text marking on the next page)

Text marking

Any activity that involves marking the text in some way such as circling, underlining, highlighting, annotating can help EAL learners to pick out the key points or important words from the rest. Some ideas:

- On a text describing a process, such as how a volcano erupts: circle all the nouns (volcano, vent, lava…) and underline all the verbs (flow, erupt, heat…)

- In a chronological account such as the Battle of Hastings: highlight all dates in yellow, people in pink and places in green

- In a description of a character from a book annotate positive words and phrases with a + and negative words and phrases with a −

Example – how does rain form?

Water droplets form from warm air. As the warm air rises it cools. When enough of these droplets collect together, they form clouds. If the clouds are big enough and have enough water droplets, the droplets come together and form even bigger drops. When the drops get heavy, they fall because of gravity, and you see and feel rain.

Key: nouns   verbs

Get it Write!

What is writing?

Speech written down?

A way of organising your thinking?

A means of communicating a message?

Handwriting?

Calligraphy?

- In some cultures calligraphy is valued as an art form
- Some people would say writing is just a written form of speech. But writing is more than this: it is a way of structuring ideas and communicating. Spoken and written language forms are not the same
- The way writing is structured follows culturally specific conventions or *genres*. (Remember GAPS on page 100.) EAL learners need to be taught the conventions of the texts commonly used in your subject

Five gold rings of writing

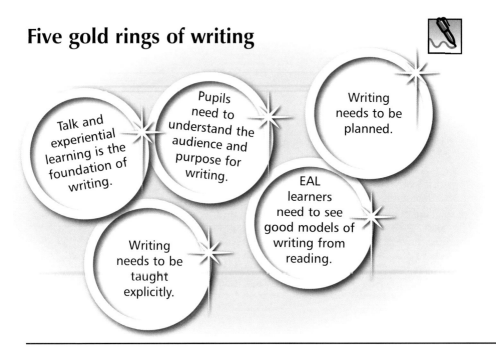

Talk and experiential learning is the foundation of writing.

Pupils need to understand the audience and purpose for writing.

Writing needs to be planned.

EAL learners need to see good models of writing from reading.

Writing needs to be taught explicitly.

Three levels of writing

We can look at writing on three levels:

Language development is not a totally linear and systematic process. EAL learners will be learning whole chunks of language through verbal interaction, not just single words. However, in planning for language development it is useful to think of a logical sequence of building language: when teaching, begin by introducing single words and then start to link words into phrases and sentences.

In this chapter you will find a range of tools for building sentences, paragraphs and creating whole texts.

Sentence makers

Sentence makers are excellent for teaching EAL learners specific structures in writing. They give pupils the opportunity to repeat and practise the language. They can be used as a scaffold for talk and to rehearse orally before writing.

Example sentence maker from Design and Technology

				wood
The	laces sole heel upper toe	is are	made of constructed from	metal plastic canvas leather rubber

Example sentences:
- The sole is constructed from rubber
- The heel is made of wood
- The upper is made of canvas
- The laces are made of leather

Heads and tails

'Heads and tails' is another great tool to help EAL learners form sentences.

Simply type out the sentences and split them in half. Copy them on to card for pupils to assemble. Think carefully about where you make the splits.

Can you match the heads and tails?

Tropical rainforests cover	rainforest in the world.
The Amazon is the largest	from rainforests.
25% of modern medicines come	7% of the earth.

Detectives and cloze

Detectives

This is a fun way of helping pupils to understand sentence grammar:

1. Prepare the sentence or sentences you want to use for teaching.
2. Tear them up into separate words or sentence parts.
3. Give pupils the 'torn up' note to reconstruct the message.
4. Identify all possibilities.

Cloze

Students have to reconstruct a text, parts of which have been deleted. You can ask them to fill in single words, titles or subheadings. Or give them subheadings and titles and ask them to add the details. You could supply the words pupils need separately or give a selection of possible words to choose from, eg:

The abstract by Van Gogh has mostly .... colours. The lines are ....

This makes you think that he is ....

Making connections

Connectives are the words that join different ideas and show the relationship between them. EAL learners need to expand their knowledge of connectives so they can express more complex thought. Here are some simple examples:

Time
First
Finally
Previously

Adding
Also
As well as
In addition

Cause and effect
So
Therefore
As a result

Difference
But
On the other hand
In contrast

Similarity
Both
Like
Similarly

Exemplifying
For example
For instance
Such as

- You could create posters and display connectives in your classroom
- You might create connectives banks for specific genres of writing
- Pupils can collect connectives and add to the lists

Making connections

Two statements:

| It rained heavily. | The river overflowed. |

Compare these sentences that link the two statements above:

The river overflowed *because* it rained heavily.
Because it rained heavily, the river overflowed.
As a result of the heavy rain, the river overflowed.
The river overflowed *as a result of* the heavy rain.

- Notice how the sentence changes depending on which connective you use
- Notice how you can change the position of some of the parts of the sentence

The implication of this is that you need to show EAL learners how to use connectives in sentences. It is not enough just to teach them the words. You could use any of the tools shown earlier in this section to do this.

Ask pupils to experiment with different connectives. How many ways can they find to link two ideas?

Sentences into paragraphs – the PEE burger

'**PEE**' – **P**oint, **E**vidence, **E**xplanation – is a useful tool to teach pupils how to build up paragraphs. Familiarise them with 'the PEE burger':

POINT Macbeth is unsure about killing King Duncan.

EVIDENCE He says, '*We will proceed no further in this business.*'

EXPLANATION He can't say the word '*murder*'. This shows he is afraid.

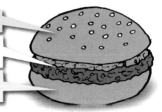

You can show pupils how to separate an example PEE paragraph like the one below:

'Swinging' is a good title for Kandinsky's painting.

He uses dynamic wavy and curved lines.

This gives a sense of movement and rhythm.

Point   Evidence   Explanation

Pupils can then use the PEE burger to build their own sentences as the basis for a longer paragraph.

Writing frames

A writing frame is a skeleton outline to scaffold pupils' writing. Writing frames can support EAL learners to write longer texts in different genres. They are useful when an EAL learner is starting to write sentences, but as students develop control over their writing the scaffold should be gradually reduced and taken away.

Writing frames can provide:
* Sentence starters
* Relevant sentence grammar
* A structure for writing
* Relevant connectives

Powerful alternatives to writing frames are modelling writing and graphic organisers (see pages 122-125).

Caution

There is a danger that writing frames can become a straitjacket rather than a support if overused.

Examples of writing frames

Discussion

There are divided views on …
Some people argue …
They claim that…
They also …
However, others would say …
In addition…
Furthermore…
Considering all of the points of view…

Interpreting results

The results of the investigation are …
From the table you can see …
This shows that …
Another interpretation could be …

Explaining evidence

This
- shows
- proves
- demonstrates
- suggests
- tells us
- illustrates

Talk frames can be used in the same way as writing frames, to scaffold talk and to practise orally before writing.

A sequence for teaching writing

The diagram below describes a powerful way of improving the writing of all pupils.
It is especially powerful for EAL learners.

Talk, Talk, Talk
Engage in experiential learning and talk to generate content for writing.

Read Together
Read examples of similar genres and talk about how they are made.

Practise At Sentence Level
Look closely at sentences and do collaborative activities to practise.

Write Together
Teacher demonstrates and models the writing, then all write together.

Write Independently
Pupils write individually or in pairs or groups and apply learning.

Review
Identify and celebrate success.

Models and modelling

Models are essential for EAL learners to know 'what a good one looks like'.

There are various ways of getting hold of and using good models of writing:
- Use examples from pupils' writing
- Use authentic 'real life' examples of the kind of text that you want pupils to write
- Compare good and bad examples of the genre
- Write them yourself!

Show pupils two good models and get them to list what they have in common. Use the tools described in the previous section of this Pocketbook (eg highlighting the features of the text) to look closely at a model and say what is good about it.

Models and modelling

While models exemplify what a good finished product looks like, modelling is a powerful way of demonstrating 'how to do it'. It shows pupils what is usually invisible by revealing what a writer is thinking during the writing process and how a final product is arrived at.

In modelling, you speak your thoughts and decisions out loud at the same time as you write.

'I want to persuade my readers that it is a bad idea, so I am going to write,
The ridiculous idea …'

The ridiculous idea…'

You can model different elements of the writing process, eg:
- Planning
- Editing and redrafting
- Composing sentences
- Linking ideas across paragraphs
- Evaluating

Graphic organisers

Graphic organisers are a great visual tool for helping students to plan and organise their writing. Some examples:

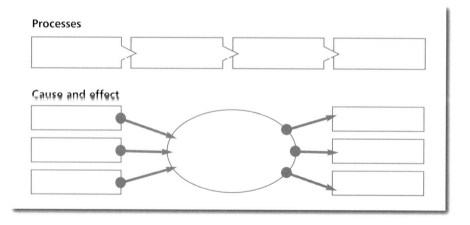

Processes

Cause and effect

Graphic organisers

Cycles

Argument

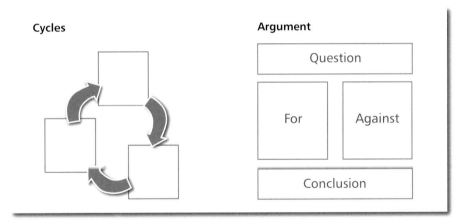

Question

For | Against

Conclusion

In summary

Students learn best when they, and their languages, are valued. Language is best learned in a meaningful context so that understanding and language are developed together.

Learning experiences for EAL learners should be cognitively challenging, and good teaching for EAL learners scaffolds learning and supports pupils to be independent.

Top Tips
1. Make your classroom a welcoming place where pupils see themselves reflected.
2. Encourage the use of first language to support learning.
3. Use visual materials to introduce topics, texts, make meaning clear and stimulate thinking and discussion.
4. Use lesson starter activities to introduce, revise and consolidate key vocabulary.
5. Create lots of opportunities for meaningful talk between peers, such as collaborative problem-solving activities.
6. Relate new learning to pupils' prior knowledge.
7. Model and demonstrate skills and techniques to be used in the lesson.
8. Provide prompts for speaking and writing activities. Have a set of blank cards handy for when unplanned-for needs arise.

Reading and websites

Ensuring the Attainment of More advanced learners of EAL CPD Modules available from www.naldic.org.uk/eal-teaching-and-learning/outline-guidance

Exploring How Texts Work
by Beverly Derewianka. Published by PETA, 1990

Learning to Learn in a Second Language by Pauline Gibbons. Published by PETA, 1998.

National Strategies Excellence and Enjoyment: learning and teaching for bilingual children in the primary years DCSF Publications, 2006

National Strategies Literacy Across the Curriculum DCSF Publications, 2001

National Strategies New Arrivals Excellence Programme DCSF Publications, 2007

Scaffolding Language Scaffolding Learning: Teaching Second Language Learners in the Mainstream Classroom by Pauline Gibbons. Published by Heinemann, 2002

Welcoming refugee children into your school An NUT teaching resource www.teachers.org.uk

www.naldic.org.uk
Information on all aspects of the teaching of English as an additional language

www.emaonline.org.uk
A wide range of information and resources

www.emas4success.org
Guidance and resources

www.collaborativelearning.org
Resources for inclusive collaborative teaching across the curriculum

www.irespect.net
Race equality and diversity resources

http://en.childrenslibrary.org
(International Children's Digital Library) *Digital books in many languages*

https://eal.britishcouncil.org/teachers/al-nexus-resources
High quality resources for all curriculum areas to support EAL learners at various levels of English fluency

http://www.twinkl.co.uk/resources/class-management/eal-esl-sen-resources
Resources aimed at primary but also suitable for pupils new to English in Secondary schools

About the author

Alice Washbourne BA (Hons), PGCE TESOL, MA Applied Linguistics, Dip Personal Coaching

Alice specialises in Literacy Across the Curriculum, EAL and teaching and learning. She believes the key to pupils' success is having enthusiastic, skilled and confident teachers. Alice works as an independent consultant and trainer and coaches teachers in developing their practice through encouraging reflection and critical self-evaluation. She is passionate about drawing out the best in teachers and learners and equality for all pupils.

Alice is an accredited Language and Literacy in Learning Across the Curriculum (LILAC) trainer and Outstanding Teaching Intervention (OTI) trainer with Osiris Educational (www.OsirisEducational.co.uk). Her previous roles include school-based EAL and Whole School Literacy Coordinator, English and Literacy Consultant for the National Strategies and Advisor for Equality and Achievement for a Local Authority.

You can contact Alice at alice@alicecoaching.co.uk or www.alicecoaching.co.uk or via LinkedIn for more information about tailor-made training, consultancy and coaching.